THE MOST
AWESOME
FACTS
FOR CURIOUS KIDS

1000+ Days of Random, Interesting & Fun Facts about Animals, Nature, Heart, Space, Science, and Much More to Inspire Young Readers

Clifford McDaniel

The information herein is offered for informational purposes solely and is universal as such. The presentation of the information is without a contract or any guarantee assurance.

The trademarks used are without any consent, and the publication of the trademark is without permission or backing by the trademark owner. All trademarks and brands within this book are for clarifying purposes only and are owned by the owners themselves, not affiliated with this document.

CONTENTS

Introduction

The world and the cool renovations we see today result from someone's curiosity. Had we all been contented with the state of the world and left things to be, we wouldn't have any of these things. We probably wouldn't be clothed. Or we would be covered in leaves and plants. There would be no means of transporting ourselves around. Moving from country to country would be exhausting on foot. Considering the high population now, we probably wouldn't even have proper hygienic means of caring for ourselves. But for curiosity, and great innovations, man has been able to advance himself and improve his life.

It is okay to be curious. Curiosity is what prunes Researchers to discover better ways of doing things. Curiosity is how scientist continues to improve human health and our surrounding. It is this same trait that got man to find more about life out there and if other lives exist in the other planetary bodies. Our curiosity has helped us know much about the Earth and its ozone layers. Now, we know how we are harming the Earth and ways to curb it. Curiosity is how technology came to be. Man's intense search for better ways to do things and come up with great innovations is applaudable.

As a child, being curious about your surroundings make you human. Everyone wants to know what is happening around them. We are conscious of what we do and how it affects us. You should be curious about the world. It's okay to want to know about the Universe and what goes on in space. Aside from the Earth are seven other planetary bodies. What happens there and are people in there are questions you may ask and talk about. Movies like superman and spaceman push your mind to the possibilities of the great things you could do. Your mind must be able to absorb these things and open up.

And the history and past events are there to guide you. to succeed, climb on the shoulders of men who have attempted it and triumphed. Listen and read up on ancient heroes and fun facts that have happened and continue to exist. Be curious about technology. As a matter of fact, nothing is more intriguing now than technology.

Curiosity helps boost your brain. It increases the brain's activities. And for every curious kid out there, fanning their flames is how we help you be better.

This book compiles the most amazing facts and fun tools for curious kids. As you read, your curiosity about certain things will become clearer. Who knows, it could also be why your flame is fanned to greatness.

The Earth

Do you know what the Earth is? You are living on Earth right now. The Earth is the planet where you live in. It is like the home for man, animals, and everything you see around. The Earth is the home for fishes, frogs, birds, elephants, pigs, insects, pests, and every animal you can imagine. The Earth also houses other living things, such as plants and microorganisms. Microorganisms are living things that cannot be seen with ordinary eyes. To see them, you need a microscope.

The Earth not only houses you and other living beings but also inanimate things such as water, stones, rock, and mountains, including things that exist in the atmosphere, like gases. Everything you see around you exists here on Earth with you.

The Earth is an amazing planet to be. Among the other planets, the Earth is still the none to support humans for so long. When you travel into space, human survival is limited. When we travel to the moon, we must take along an oxygen tank to breathe. If not, we would die out there in less than two minutes. The Earth is the only planet that provides man with the basic need of life. Our basic needs include water, oxygen, and food. To survive out there, we must take our essential needs.

There are eight planets, and the Earth is the third planet from the Sun. The first to the Sun is Mercury, then Venus, followed by Earth.

These first three planets are sometimes called the Rocky planets because they have lots of rock in them. They are also different from the other planets in these rocky constituents. Planets like Jupiter, Saturn, Uranus, and Neptune are called gassy planets. They are mostly made of gases. The eight planets are far, about as much as 50,000km, and they move around the Sun at different times, so they don't collide.

The Earth being the third planet away from the Sun, may be one of its blessings. This is because it places the Earth safely from the Sun, which is very hot. The distance makes it possible for water and every basic need of man to exist without interference from the Sun. So, the Earth is not too hot like Venus, nor is it too unbearably cold like Mars. It is just the right amount of everything, a perfect blend!

It is from this perfection that the Earth got its name. For a long while, different cultures battled for the right name for the perfect planet. The Greeks named it _Gaia_ after their titanic entity. They saw the Earth as the 'Mother Earth.' The Romans believe the word 'mother' better represents the Earth. As for the Romans, they saw the Earth as _Tello_.

Earth is a name coined by the Tellus goddess of soil fertility. While the other planets were named after Greek and Roman gods, the Earth remains Eventually, they came together when they realized they had both named the Earth just right. This goddess is believed to be the god of soil fertility. The name Earth itself dates back a thousand years. And it means; the sphere of mortal life as distinguished from the sphere of spirit life.

There is one cool fact about the Earth still. When you look at the sky, what do you see? There are different kinds of birds, Eagle, Sparrow, and Vulture. Lots of them. There are also Jet, airplane, and other flying objects. Have you wondered how these things work and do not fall? What is keeping everything and everyone in check? Why aren't we falling off? It's because there is much more to the Earth.

Here are fun facts to know about the Earth:

Gravity

First, let's understand why those flying beings and objects don't fall off the sky. There is a simple answer to this. Something holds everyone down here and keeps everyone up there. That thing that keeps everyone in their place is a force. There are several forces, but the one that keeps people walking and not falling off, the force that keeps the birds to continue flying and not drop off, that force is called Gravity.

It is amazing how the force of Gravity works. While the force of Gravity keeps everyone where they should be and does not fall off, it also makes sure whatever goes out of its place comes back to stay. Yes, the force of Gravity has a simple rule; *__whatever goes up must come down.__* That is what happens when you throw up a ball. The ball goes up until the force of Gravity decides it's time to go down. And then the pen starts to fall back down.

The force of Gravity can do this using the weight of that object. If your ball weighs 2g, Gravity produces a downward force that can bring down that weight. The force of Gravity was discovered by Sir Isaac Newton three centuries ago (300 years ago). He discovers the force while enjoying the evening breeze in his garden. He had a nice time when suddenly an apple dropped. Sir Newton became intrigued. He wanted to know what made the apple fall since no one had gone near it. This makes him start his research and learn about this incident. And so he discovered that there exists a force on Earth that keeps everything in check. He would also find out that this same force pulls down objects thrown up.

Here are more cool facts about this force:

We all evert the force of Gravity around us. As long as an object has mass, it can exert Gravity's force on objects around it. Humans exert the force of Gravity on each other. This force is weaker and has no catastrophic effect because humans have large body masses almost equal to each other. The gravitational force that two bodies exert on each other is proportional to their masses. This force here is hard to detect between bodies with similar masses.

Big objects exert bigger Gravity. An object that weighs more has a bigger force of Gravity than a smaller object. Unlike the Sun, the moon is smaller than the Earth.

The force of Gravity isn't the same on all planets: The force of Gravity varies from planet to planet. While some are higher than the Earth's force of Gravity, some are relatively lower. The force of Gravity depends on the mass of a body. A body with no mass has no force of Gravity to exert. While the force of Gravity on Earth is 10m/s2

On Mercury, the force of Gravity is 3.7m/s2, and the mass is 3.30 x 1023kg. Venus' force of Gravity is 8.87m/s2. The moon has the least gravitational pull of 1.62m/s2.

Mass is not the same as Weight; The mass of an object is different from what it weighs. Mass is also not a force. When you want to measure force, you measure in Newton (N). You measure weight and mass in Kilogram (kg) or gram (g). So, how, then, can we tell each apart?

Let's go back to that ball you threw up earlier. What if you open the ball to know what is in there? And how about you have the same ball of the same size? Two balls. Now each ball might be the same size. But when you decide to open up the balls, you can see that each ball carries different things. Why is one heavy with materials that it contains, and the other can be light since it has no heavy materials inside? The materials inside that ball that make it heavy or light are called mass. It is these materials (mass) that will then determine the weight of that object.

Your body mass doesn't change. If your body mass is 20kg and you decide to go on a trip to the moon. Your body mass remains 20kg. If, however, you weigh 50 pounds on Earth, on another planet, your body weight can be lesser or higher depending on the force of Gravity on that planet. Mars, for instance, has a lesser force of Gravity than Earth. So, your weight becomes lesser when you travel to Mars. Your body mass, however, remains the same across these planets.

Black holes have the strongest gravitational pull. Black holes are open spaces that light cannot penetrate, hence their name; black holes. These holes can't be seen since light penetrating them isn't possible. We only see these holes using space telescopes. They have a very intense gravitational force field. The force of Gravity in black holes is so strong because huge matter has been squeezed into a tiny space due to a dying star.

The result of this is gravitational energy that, though it can't be seen the effect is visible. The air around black holes and stars are pointer to this.

The smallest black hole is called a Stellar, formed at the center of a big star. It happens when this big star collapses on itself. Supernovas are the effect of Stellar. A supernova is an exploding star caused by small black holes (stellar). The supernova blasts through another star and causes a part of it to enter space. The biggest black hole is called supermassive. These big black holes have large masses began than even the Sun. Supermassive is also proven to be seen in large galaxies. Earth only has

Black holes sound scary, but they do not go around swallowing up everything in their path. Understandably, we want to know if black holes exist on Earth. Thankfully no, the Earth is geographically too far from black holes to be sucked in. Even if the black hole has a mass bigger than the Sun or takes up the place of the Sun, it still will not happen. As it rotates around the Sun, the Earth naturally rotates around the black hole.

The moon's Gravity causes ocean tides: when you stroll at the beach, everything looks beautiful, the serene water and bright atmosphere. Suddenly, when you see the ocean rise, roll forward, and fall back. The rise and fall of water are what is called ocean tide. Ocean tides happen because of the force of Gravity or the gravitational pull effect of the Earth and moon. The force of Gravity makes it in such a way that all bodies in the Universe pull towards and on each other. This explains why both the Sun and moon pull on the Earth. However, the moon has a larger pull on Earth due to its closeness to the Earth. When the moon pulls on the Earth, it makes the water move. You can observe this movement on two sides; the side of the Earth closest to the moon when the pull happens. The movement is also seen on the side of the Earth farthest from the moon during the pull. This movement is what results in the highs and low tides. It is easy to know which tide comes from the moon's force and Earth's force. The moon causes high and low tides, also known as tides. The highest level that the ocean rises to is called the high tide. The low tides are the ocean's lowest level when it falls back down. At least two high and low tides happen daily. But though we can be sure two highs and low tides happen daily, when they happen can't be pinpointed. The time changes from day to day. Scientists have also been able to measure the time apart. When a tide happens like now, the next tide takes about 12 hours and 20-30 minutes before happening.

No one can feel the force of Gravity. The effects, however, are undeniable: The force of Gravity isn't something we feel. It's an experience we see, though. You can see the ball falling but do not see the force pulling it back to Earth. We can see the birds flapping their wings but cannot see the force it takes to keep it up in the sky. We see the cool effects.

Earth's Shape and Size

The Earth is not a flat surface. If it were, we would be falling off the Earth. So, what is the shape of this planet? Think of it this way – eight planets are rotating around the Sun. What shape could they be for them to move around the Sun? Taking a large chunk of snow and balling it into a circle isn't perfect. Then take smaller chunks to make circular shapes, flat, rectangular, and triangles. The big circular chunk represents the Sun. The smaller shapes are the planets. Will the flat shapes rotate? Maybe not! Neither will the squares and triangles.

The only ones that rotate will be the circular chunks.

Suffice it to say that the Earth, including the other planets, is circular. They are not perfectly round but spherical shapes. This discovery was made by Christopher Columbus, dating back to the 14th century. This happened when he decided to tour the whole world. His journey wasn't aimed at discovering the shape of the Earth because it has always been believed that the Earth is at least round. This discovery dates back thousands of years back. In 1942, Columbus set sail. He had it in mind that his ship would land in Asia. Since he was certain the Earth was round, he sailed west instead of East. He reasoned that since the Earth was round, he would eventually reach his destination. He did. Not just that, he also discovered a new world no one knew existed. Columbus created many, which was his main intention when he set out on the journey. He may not have proven an already known fact, but he did discover something new. And unlike stories passed down from the

Greeks, his journey showed what everyone already knew and not some folklore stories.

The layers of the Earth

The Earth is a constituent of its atmosphere, layers, and surface. The atmosphere is the protective covering for the Earth. It keeps the Earth shielded from radiation penetrating through. The atmosphere doesn't only protect the Earth from harmful Ultraviolet rays but also serves as a shield for everything that exists in it. Without the atmosphere, the Earth wouldn't exist. That is how important the atmosphere is to the Earth. The atmosphere keeps the temperatures of day and night of the Earth and comprises layers of gases. It is what keeps us from inhaling dangerous gases that the Sun emits.

Several things make up the atmosphere. These include the gases which are crucial to both man and plants. Oxygen is one of the gases that make up the atmosphere. It is the oxygen that we breathe in and what keeps us alive. Another important gas that makes up the atmosphere is carbon dioxide which is extremely important to plants' survival. While we need oxygen to stay alive, plants also need carbon dioxide for survival. As important as these two gases are, they are not the main component of the Earth's atmosphere. The largest constituent of the atmosphere. Oxygen takes up about 21% of the atmospheric gas, while carbon dioxide gets 0.04%. That is less than 1% of the atmospheric gas. Nitrogen takes up 78% of the atmosphere. Others include argon which takes up 0.93%, and other trace elements like hydrogen, helium, neon, methane, krypton, and water vapor. The atmosphere is composed of five layers. Each of these layers serves its unique purpose. They are:

1. ***Troposphere:*** when you lift your face at the sky, the upper surface of the Earth that you can see is the troposphere. The troposphere is the layer concerned with keeping plants protected. To do this, the shallow layer troposphere needs to get the air plants need for their photosynthesis intact. You should know what the name means to understand what happens in the troposphere. Troposphere was coined from the word *'tropos.'* Tropos means change. And change is exactly what happens in this layer. Gases are continuously mixing up in this layer. It also contains 95-98% water vapor and aerosols. The troposphere doesn't cover much of the Earth. It extends to 8-12 kilometers and is the closest to the Earth. It also the thickest atmosphere. Troposphere is the layer that dictates the weather and most of the atmospheric conditions like rain, snow, and drizzles. The exception to this is thunderclouds. The thunderclouds have tops that reach the next atmospheric layer (stratosphere). About 75% of the air in the atmosphere is found in the troposphere.

2. ***Stratosphere:*** this layer is the next layer directly above the troposphere. It is about 50 kilometers away from the Earth's surface. This is the layer popularly known as the ozone layer. The ozone layer is the one that protects us from the ultraviolet ray of the Sun. The Ultraviolet ray from the Sun heating this layer

makes it warm as you go higher. The stratosphere is mostly cloudy and doesn't dictate the weather much. It, however, sometimes has a polar stratospheric cloud present in its low and cold altitudes. This is the highest layer of the Earth that the airplane can reach. So, the next time you see a plane flying, you can tell which layer in the atmosphere it is. You can also tell how hot or warm that layer is.

3. **Mesosphere:** the mesosphere is the immediate layer above the stratosphere. This layer is about 80 kilometers above the Earth and is mostly cold. As you go higher into this layer, it gets colder. Its average temperature is 85 degrees Celsius. Water vapor, which is rarely seen in the mesosphere, forms the noctilucent cloud. This cloud is the highest that the human eye can see. And even this is not all the time. It happens under certain conditions. The upper part of the mesosphere is called mesopause. The coldest part of the Earth's atmosphere is the mesopause. Rockets and aircraft can reach this layer of the Earth. Jets and balloons do not get to the mesosphere.

4. **Thermosphere**: The thermosphere comes after the mesosphere. It covers between 78-700 kilometers above the Earth's surface. Its lowest part contains the ionosphere. This layer contains neither water vapor nor clouds. The temperature here increases as you go higher because of the low density of the molecules

present in the thermosphere. The low air density makes it easy to call it outer space.

5. **_Exosphere:_** the exosphere is 700-10,000 kilometers above the Earth's surface. It is also the highest layer of the Earth. The highest point of this layer wings into the solar. The layer has low density because of the molecules. This makes it not act like gas, thus allowing its particles to escape into space. A higher percentage of satellite orbit in this layer. This layer consists of hydrogen and helium that are widely spread and do not collide.

The Earth's surface

For the most part, when talking about the atmosphere, we kept mentioning the Earth's surface. The Earth's surface is the part above. The Earth's surface is covered in water. 70% of the Earth's surface is made up of water, with the remaining 30% made up of land. Out of the 70% water content, the ocean makes up about 95% of this. Water exists in every part of the Earth. It is in the air we breathe as water vapor. And the remaining part of the Earth, which is land, even has some water. It exists in the water as moisture. And you know something amazing? Even if you have water in you, including your pets.

The majority of the water on Earth's surface is saline water. Saline water is salty water. This explains why the ocean is salty. Aside from saline water, there is fresh water. Fresh water is the water that comes from the sky (as rainfall). It then moves into streams, oceans, lakes, and rivers.

Water exists in the ground. And such water is very important to life. Much more water remains under the ground. Underground water makes up some of the flowing rivers.

The Earth's Age

The Earth's Age: The Earth is billions of years old. The Earth is believed to have been over 4 billion years old. This is in contrast to the living being that life on Earth. Human age is researched to date back to 300,000 years. This means the Earth existed billion years ago before humans began living there. How cool is that? What do you think it was like for the first human on Earth?

The Earth's size: the Earth is so small compared to the size of the Sun. When you look at the sky, it appears like the Sun is small, but it isn't. The Earth is quite smaller than the Sun. As a matter of fact, the Sun can hold millions of Earths in it. Yes, the Sun is that much bigger!

Historical Moments

Historical moments are times in the past when man experienced an event for the first time. Sometimes, it might not be the first experience but the beauty with which such incidence occurs. Historical moments are preserved, and the stories are told from generation to generation. And man has been blessed with lots of memorable incidences, including the firsts of many things.

Moon Walking

Humans have always been fascinated by the moon and what life exists there. Severally, we have tried to travel down to the moon to see what goes on there. Though the attempts weren't successful, they were not a failure either. Each mission was a discovery of what could be done better. And the next missions after it was improved based on the last obstacle. The earliest attempts to see the moon happened in 1968. Astronauts Wally Schirra, Donn Eisele, and Walt Cunningham were the first to go on the moon landing attempt. Their mission was to know how long it would take to get to the moon and back. The team stayed in the Earth's orbit for 11 days. Though the machines and technology were fine, the crew weren't. They fell ill after spending a day on their flight. A cold broke out, and it wasn't a good experience when almost weightless in the sky.

NASA, in explaining having a cold in the air said it was the worst. *"Mucus accumulates, fills the nasal passages, and doesn't drain from the head."* There was no relief until you blew out the mucous and hard too. This would, of course, have a dreadful effect on the ear drums. The simple explanation was that it's different when you are cold here, on Earth. You allow need to get some pain killers, do a steam bath, and you are good. The cold could run for days, or weeks, but the effect isn't so alarming. In space, cold is another story. The mucus piles up in the nostrils, blocking entrance. Breathing becomes difficult. There is no way to be better unless you blow the mucus out. The annoying thing about doing that is blowing isn't just done casually. You must blow with the force of getting out the accumulated mucus. The force of blowing painfully affects the ears. Cold in space is a terrible thing!

After the Apollo 7 attempt, Apollo 8 launched in December of the same year. The mission aimed at getting into space, not just the Earth's orbit. This made the team, Frank Borman, Jim Lovell, and Williams Anders, the first human to travel outside the Earth's orbit. They went as far as seeing the back of the moon for 68 hours. This team made the iconic discovery of the Earth showing up in the moon space. While they were in space, to their surprise, the crew saw the Earth approaching. It was a monumental event. They discovered what is now known as the Earthrise. A phenomenon that explains Earth's appearance in space.

Other missions happened to further smoothen the first successful journey to the moon. Apollos 9, and 10 were launched. Then finally, it was time to moonwalk. And Neil A. Armstrong was the man for the job.

Perhaps one needs to know more about Neil to understand what great feat this man did and how he achieved it. Born in Ohio on August 5, 1930, Neil had an eye out for a career in NASA. He served as a Naval Aviator for three years, dating from 1949-1952. He later joined the National Committee for Aeronautics (NACA) in 1955. There, Neil started to build his career. He worked on his career for seventeen years, going from Engineer to becoming a test pilot, Astronaut, and finally, NACA administrator. He was part of the team when the successor agency, NASA came on board on October 1, 1958.

Neil was a research pilot for NASA (National Aeronautics Space Administrator). Along with the team, he worked on several high-speed aircraft. He piloted over 200 airplanes ranging from jets, rockets, helicopters, and gliders. Seeing that he had accomplished enough, Neil transferred to Astronaut in 1962. He was a command pilot for Gemini 8. And on March 16, 1966, he successfully docked two vehicles in space.

In 1969, another attempt to get to the moon was launched. The mission was named; Apollo 11. Twelve (12) men were gathered for this mission, including Neil A. Armstrong and Edwin Aldrin. On July 21, Neil Armstrong, and his team, embarked on another trip to the moon. And this time, it was a successful journey. At exactly 2:56 GMT, Neil stepped out of the craft and walked on the moon. He walked on the part of the moon named the *'sea of tranquility.'* It was a great feat for humankind. NASA capturing his triumphant report said Neil was excited. He reported the instant he placed his feet on the moon. His exact words were, "That's one small step for man, one giant leap for mankind." What do you think Neil meant?

Neil saw his stepping on the moon as a seemingly small achievement personally. But even that wasn't. Imagine being the first human to step on the man? He couldn't believe his small feet was stepping on such monumental space. The small feat was going to be historical for humanity. Not only did this move show that humans can walk on the moon, but it also opened up the possibility that we can do more than take small leaps into the moon. And reporting back to NASA, Neil said, "Houston, Tranquility Base here. The Eagle has landed."

Seeing the bold move by his partner, Aldrin stepped out of the lunar module that transported them to the moon to join his friend. It took him 19 minutes to decide if he wanted to take that risky step. And once he stepped on the moon, like Neil, Aldrin was awestruck. They took samples of the moon to take back to Earth and photographs. They also made a video recording which they transmitted back to NASA. A video that went viral with over 500 million views. In all, Neil and Aldrin spent two hours on the moon.

In August 2012, Neil Armstrong died of heart complications in Cincinnati. But even the world couldn't forget him. In honor of his memory, NASA had an asteroid and lunar crater after him. Other schools and museums were named Armstrong in memory of the first man to walk the moon.

After the first moonwalkers, several other attempts have been made to reach the moon. NASA has launched several Apollo missions since Apollo 11. Apollo 12 mission, led by Pete Conrad and Alan Bean, was a success. Mission 13, however, proved different as one of the oxygen tanks exploded after two days. The mission had to be aborted. However, Jim Lovell and Fred Haise set a different record as the farthest humans have come from Earth. Several other successful missions were launched, which include; Apollo 14 mission by Alan Shepard and Edgar Mitchell. Apollo 15 was led by David Scott and James Irwin. Apollo 16 John Young and Charles Duke. Apollo 17 Gene Cernan and Harrison Schmitt. In total, about fourteen men have been to the moon.

How long it takes to get to the moon

Traveling to the moon from Earth is determined by different factors. However, the distance between the Earth to the moon is estimated at around 250-260,000 miles. For the first crew (Apollo 11), it took them 04:06:45:00 days. That's four (4) days, six (6) hours, and forty-five (45) minutes to get to the moon. There have been better improvement since Apollo 11 went on their mission. Now, there are cooler, faster ways to get to the moon.

The New Horizons Probe, launched by NASA on January 19, 2006, was the fastest flight to the moon. This spacecraft takes just 8 hours and 35 minutes to get past the moon to Pluto.

The last moonwalkers

Apollo 17 mission ended the moon walking trips. Eugene Carman and Harrison Schmitt led this team in December 1972. These crews explored and collected samples on the lunar outer space for seven hours. Then they explored the inner lunar space and explored for another 10-11 hours. These men spent almost a day enjoying the lunar space. They are, till now, the last men to have walked the moon.

The moon doesn't have an atmosphere, so there is no water, no air. There is no water to wash off anything. This means that the footprints of the moonwalkers will be forever imprinted on the moon. At least, for a million years those footprints would be on the moon. What an indelible mark! Footprints on the moon!

As silent as the Space!

The space is a large body of surface, vacuum where the planets and other celestial objects are located. The space is another one place that man is fully yet to explore. There is so much to the space that we do not know. Yet, man has been able to learn a lot about it. And from what vast knowledge man has gathered, there are cool discoveries about the space what being curious about.

❖ There's no sound to be heard in space! We have sound on Earth because there is an atmosphere. The space has no atmosphere and at such allows for no sound to penetrate. So, maybe the next time you want to complete the phrase as silent as a... you might want to add- space!

- ❖ Venus is one of the planetary bodies in space. It has a slow axis that takes it 243 days to make a complete day on Earth. This means that a day on Venus is close to a year on Earth. If you decide to live in Venus, you'd be younger when you get back. If you stayed there for three days, by the time you come back to Earth, your agemates would be two and a half year older than you!

- ❖ The space holds many stars. These stars are so many you can't count them all. Making an attempt to count the stars is like trying to count the grains of sand on Earth.

- ❖ The space is a cold welder! No two metals can meet in space. If they do, they will stick together for eternity. This is called cold welding, and space does a lot of that.

- ❖ Of the eight planets, Mercury and Venus have no moon. The space has 176 moons, yet Mercury and Venus have none. How sad! Those two would be looking at the other planets and wondering what's that beautiful light that shines through at night. They would be green with envy. Amazingly, one of the planets has twenty-seven moons. None other than Uranus wears that crown.

- ❖ Mars holds the highest mountain ever discovered. The mountain Olympus Mons is the highest known mountain. Its peak is 26km high, 374, 015 feet squared, and is thrice the height of Mount Everest.

How sunny and hot!

The sun is the flaming hot circular object at the center of the Solar System. It radiates energy as ultraviolet, infrared, and light. The sun hits the Earth with the energy ever hour. As extremely hot as it is, the sun is the energy source of life for Earth. Plants and animals rely on the sun for food, growth and oxygen. Humans need plant to produce oxygen. Without oxygen, we'd all die. Sun provides us with that. For plants to grow, they need the sunlight. Animals also need the plant to grow so they can eat. So, the sun is at the center of every living being's survival.

Aside from this, the sun is also beneficial to Earth. It isn't just the Earth's occupant who benefit from it. The sun keeps the Earth from freezing. Without the sun thawing the Earth, it would freeze over, along with everything in it. That yellowish dwarf star is really a life saver!

The sun is 4.5 billions of years old. It is yellowish star dwarf, made up of hydrogen fused together to create helium. The fusion is a nuclear fusion. Hydrogen takes up about three quarter of the sun while Helium takes up the remain one quarter.

❖ The sun is the hottest body in space. The temperature is as high as 450 degree centigrade. This makes the closest planet to it so hot. What planet do you think is the closest to the sun? yes, it's Mercury. But Mercury isn't the hottest planet. Venus is. What could be the explanation behind this? Here is what goes on up there. Mercury like the space has no atmosphere. The atmosphere doesn't allow sound to penetrate. It also doesn't have a way to regulate its temperature all thanks to the no-atmosphere syndrome. This makes the planet (Mercury) become irregular. The attention thus goes to Venus, the next planet to it. And so, Venus claimed the title of the hottest planet.

❖ The sun is much bigger than the Earth. Its body mass is 300,000 times more than that of Earth's. This means the sun can swallow up a million and one Earth without an issue. Thankfully, it isn't a black hole and cannot swallow the Earth. The sun also takes up almost the entire space in the solar system, occupying about 99.9%.

❖ In Mars, the sunset is blue when you are gazing from the red planet.

Inventing the Internet

Over the years, humans have begun to understand the world and invent new things too. The invention of the internet, where you have access to its wealth of knowledge, dates centuries back. At least the search began then. People consider January 1, 1983, as the official birth date of the internet. Before this, computers, though big, been built. The first computer, named ENIAC, was built in 1945. It was room sized. After that, more computers were built. And as computer scientists continue improving their model, the size started to reduce. Now we have laptops, tablets, and phones.

With computers springing forth, scientists began to look for a way to connect these computers. The connection between computers is how the INTERNET came to be. As always, several people came around to figure out a solution. Many scientists, researchers, programmers, engineers, and developers tried to think of a way around this. As each came up with a discovery, another proposed a way forward. And together, they started to devise a means to accomplish this.

Before even technology came into existence, there was speculation that there needed to be a way to link people from all works of life. In the early 1900s, *Nikola Tesla* proposed a world wireless system. The idea fascinated Paul Otlet and Vannevar Bush. They propose that the wireless system be stored with mechanized books and media that are available when searched for. And for years, work began in earnest to birth this great magic.

However, nothing happened until the late 90s. In 1960, the first internet schematics were announced. The inventor, MIT's J.C.R Licklider, popularized the idea of linking computers. Something that makes it possible to use one computer here and access it miles away from a different computer. The idea wasn't swept under the rug or seen as an impossible dream. Rather, computer scientists began to work on a way that allows for switching packets. The idea works like a way to transmit information from one computer to another. That way, one can access one's data at any point in time from separate computers.

The project, funded by the United States Department of Defense, was a success in 1969. Advanced Research Projects Agency Network, known as ARPANET, was birth. ARPANET made it possible for communication among multiple computers on a single network. To test this project, two computers were placed in different locations. The first one was put in a research laboratory at UCLA. The second one was put in Stanford. The first computers made then big that they each were the size of a small house. There was no fancy tablet or chip then. There weren't even laptops.

The test on ARPANET begins with the communication message "LOGIN." It was the shortest message ever. And the first of its kind. Scientists, and developers jubilated with triumph. But their victory was cut short when the system crashed. ARPANET proved that communication between computers was possible. The researchers only needed to do more.

The 1970s were marked by research and further developments in computer communication. Robert Kahn and Vinton Cerf developed Transmission Control Protocol and Internet Protocol. This communications model allowed data to be transmitted between computer networks.

In 1983, ARPANET was test-run using the Transmission Control that Robert and Vinton developed. It worked just fine. It gave room for computer assemblers to build on it. By 1990, the world wide web was looking more like it. Tim Berners-Lee invented the world wide web, and people loved it. For a while, though, people were confused about the difference between these two. And so, the world web was mistaken for the internet.

The world wide web made it possible to access data as websites and links on the internet. The web also increased the fame of the internet to the public. And we have unlimited access to information on the internet today because of the web.

With scientists and researchers focusing now on world wed, attention wasn't completely lost on the internet. On October 1, 1957, the first artificial satellite was launched. The satellite, named SPUTNIK, was launched into orbit. All Sputnik did was a few bleeps here and there. And it was the next best exciting thing. Sputnik was able to circle the Earth. As it moved, it was bleeping with its radio transmitter. Sputnik's movement and invention by the Soviet Union was an eye-opener into a world of possibilities where science and technology could do far more.

Science and technology started to gain the world's attention. Schools began to see the need to add science subjects to courses to be taught in classes. Corporate bodies sort help from the government to run research in this field. Of course, this was an idea the federal government willingly funded. As the discoveries and innovations began to spring forth, the government itself formed her agency. The agency formed to get more knowledge on science and technology was named NASA. National Aeronautics and Space Administration wasn't the only agency the government formed. Advanced Research Projects Agency (ARPA) is another agency that works for the government on scientific research. These agencies together developed cool technologies such as computers in smaller sizes, rockets, and defense tools, including ARPANET.

ARPANET was born to show that communication between computers was possible. Further advancement in technology. The first attempt involved only two computers, and the connection broke off after the first word: LOGIN. But by 1969, four computers were successfully linked. And the internet connection started to grow from there. By 1971, the four communicating computers grew to include other computers. So much so that, ALOHAnet was added.

ALOHAnet is Hawaii University's computer. The university was able to add their computer to the linked computer, further showing that more computers can be connected. London's University College saw this and signed up for her computer. It was another success, and scientists couldn't be prouder. The Royal Radar Establishment in Norway also decided to join the connection. And so, the connection grew. The connections grew so much that integrating them into a singular worldwide internet became a hassle. And another invention had to be sorted.

Computer scientist Vinton Cerf began his research into a probable solution to this. He came up with Transmission Control Protocol, also known as Internet Protocol. The singular purpose of the TCP was to make sure there could be the safe connection between computers. The transmission protocol was to make sure not even distance was a barrier. And that births the virtual space connection.

The internet continues to grow from the connections into a worldwide network. The 1980s was a tremendous moment for humans. The internet was used to send files, data, and information from one computer to another. No longer was there the need to wait endlessly for letters or emails to arrive. It was a soothing relief. As much as this was a great feat, scientists knew it could be improved. It became urgent to improve on it when emails were being intercepted and some lost.

The internet as we know it

A computer programmer, Tim Berners-Lee from Switzerland, introduced the world wide web. The idea was to have computers transmit information safely. The web did more than that. Like a library of information, the web was a wealth of resources. Tim introduced us to the modern-day internet as we know it today.

Researchers have continued to build on and improve the internet. Using the resources available already, researchers from the University of Illinois 1992 built a browser. They named it Mosaic, which later was renamed **Netscape**. The browser allowed users to search for words, and images and use scrollbars and clicks to navigate. Later that year, the web was discovered to be possible for commercial use. Companies started to engage programmers to build their websites. And today, we have lots of those around. Companies leveraged the internet and started to make sales from anywhere in the world.

And finally, it was only about making just sales. Social networking websites started to spring up. And there began the emergence of social networking sites such as Facebook, Twitter, and LinkedIn where people could easily connect.

And should anyone ask who made the internet, you can see that no one did. The internet is the work of great minds and researchers.

Queens has two birthdays

How many times do you celebrate your birthday in a year? Everyone celebrates their birthdays once, because we only have one birth date. The day we were born. Do you know this is not the same for the Queen of England? The Queen celebrates her birthday twice every year. What does this mean? That she was given birth to twice? Or that this is the tradition. The interesting thing is there is a stipulated day for this event.

Queen Elizabeth celebrates her birthdays in April and June. The April birthday is celebrated every 21st and earmarked with a hundred and four (104) gun salutes. Twenty-one (21) gun salutes will each be fired at the Winsor great park and Hyde park. The remaining sixty-two (62) salutes will be fired at the Tower of London. This is done every April 21 to celebrate the Queen of England.

There is a rule, however that forbids the firing of the gun on Sundays. This overrules the Queen's celebratory salute. So, if the Queen's birthday on the 21st happens to be on a Sunday, the guns will not be fired. Instead, the gun salutes would be fired the following Monday. And that ends the Queen's first birthday for the year.

The second birthday happens in June. This is the Queen's official birthday. The official birthday isn't the real birthday. It is just a date picked to celebrate the Queen.

The story behind the Queen's legendary birthdays.

Back in the day, England was ruled by kings. The King who laid out this tradition was King George, born in 1968-1760. When the British weather was unpredictable, the King George couldn't tell from the weather which date was his actual birthdate. There was also no calendar to help. All he knew was that he was given birth in November. To save himself from the trouble of dates, he earmarked his birthdate by a historical moment in the state. That was a smart move. That way, whenever this public event was celebrated, he knew it was his birthdate too. He thus celebrated his birthday yearly during the Trooping of color in summer. An event that is still celebrated now. This occasion is marked by a procession of military men, the band of musicians, and horses that matches from Buckingham Palace to the Horse Guards Parade.

Thus, it became a standing rule to have to celebrate monarchs. One was the official date which is the second Saturday in June. And the main birthday is celebrated on the day the Queen was born. For queen Elizabeth, her actual birthday is April 21. The official date is that celebrated in June. What this means is that every Queen is celebrated in June, their actual birth month. This tradition has been observed for generations.

Amazing things to know about Queen Elizabeth II

- Queen Elizabeth Alexandra Mary was born on April 21, 1926. She was given birth to in Mayfair, London. At the time of her birth, she was not in line for the throne. Her uncle, the King in 1936, abdicating the throne and placed Queen Elizabeth's father on the throne. The Queen then became the next in line. When her father died in 1952, Princess Elizabeth became the Queen at age 25. She passed on the September 8, 2022.

- The Queen was fourteen years old when she had her first radio speech. She wasn't a queen yet, then.
- The Queen was the only one who could drive in the United Kingdom without a driving license.
- She was the longest-ruling monarch. Queen Elizabeth II became the Queen of England when she was twenty-five years old. She ruled for seventy years and died at 96 years of age.
- The Queen has sovereignty immunity. What it means is she cannot be prosecuted for anything. This made her the most powerful individual in the world. She could have misused her power. Instead, she is known to care genuinely for her citizens, which got her the tag; "Mother of nations." Her interest in politics and the major roles that she played remained astonishing.
- Fourteen prime ministers served her. One of her ministers was the infamous Churchill Winston.
- Queen Elizabeth's reign was marked by many impressive deeds. She brought stability, modernized the monarch, and played a great role in transforming the commonwealth, amongst others.

Ancient Egyptians and the Christmas tree

There is something sweet about Christmas. You may not be able to place your fingers on it, but something about Christmas intrigues everyone. Perhaps the mood, the beautiful snowy weather, or it's the song. Everyone knows when it's Christmas. Red and green colors flash all over the city. And when the Christmas tree comes out, it's the holiday season again.

Christmas is celebrated, and the tradition is passed down from generation to generation. And no, it's not what you think. Christmas as we know it wasn't as it was back then. For one, December 25 wasn't always Christmas day. It was a day Romans celebrated the birth of their sun god, Mithra.

With the introduction of Christianity came some significant changes. Rather than celebrating their gods, Christian clergy was able to adopt this celebration from the pagans. So, December 25 was named the day Jesus was born. As such, the actual birthdate of Jesus Christ was lost to everyone. And December 25 became the Savior's official birthdate.

Christmas Tree

The story behind the Christmas trees dates back to ancient Egypt. Egyptians and Romans are known for their symbolic love for greens. During winter, plants and trees stayed green. And usually, when people decorate, they pluck the greens and take them in. Some preserved the plants and placed them in bowls with soil, so they continued growing. Others used them as pruned flowers and decorations. Aside from the decoration, spiritual folks take the greens to be more. They saw these plants as something that drove off evil spirits. And so, they would cut the green plants and hang them on their doors and walls to protect them from evil and illnesses.

Green also means fertility. For people who saw no link to hanging trees on their ways to drive off evil, they saw greens as healthy. So, even if the trees weren't for diabolical use, they still represented something that could stand for. When the idea of using trees as Christmas decorations, was readily welcomed, albeit for varying reasons.

The Germans started the use of lighted Christmas trees during Christmas. Egyptians, Rome, and America soon adopted it. And then, everyone started to welcome the idea from New England to several other countries. There was just a problem. The problem was separating pagan implications from this tradition, especially for Christians. People like Oliver Cromwell stood against the idea. To this class of thinkers, using Christmas trees and others were pagan practice. It stood against everything the doctrine of Christianity and the true meaning of Christmas.

Eventually, in 1659, the law had to step in. The law (General Court of Massachusetts) forbade any form of decoration on December 25. It ruled that only church services should hold on to Christmas day. Residents were penalized and made to pay a fine for hanging trees in their homes. People refrained from decorating their homes for fear of being fined. Those who decorated were selective about who entered their home. This sad period continued until the mid-18s.

A picture of Queen Victoria and her family standing close to a Christmas tree found its way into the papers in 11846. Because she was popular and well-celebrated, no one saw the office. Rather, people saw the beauty and fashion sense in it. Gradually, the Christmas tree season arrived. And by the 1890s, people were decorating their homes again. From mere trees from the garden, the Christmas tree grew into ornamental decorated trees by the Americans. From there, Germans introduced lighted trees.

Amazing Animals on Earth

Animals make for great company and pets. Besides, these are amazing creatures, and there's so much to know about them. Every animal has something interesting about them. Sometimes, their interesting attribute might be their adaptation skill like the birds who hop and leave the country for another in search of a fair livelihood. There are those animals with really weird facts about them, and some have captivating features. Cheetahs, for instance, are pretty fast cats. They cover miles up to 70 in an hour. Their speed helps them get food on their table, as their prey cannot outrun them.

There's the royal butterfly too. These are widely known as the monarch butterfly. Every year, the monarch butterfly takes a trip. Their breeding ground is in North America. However, the colorful insects take a vacation every year. They travel as far as Mexico in mass. And if you think only the chameleon camouflages, think again. Several others, like the octopus, do too. As for the animals you do not know exist, here are some.

Animals you don't know exist

Researchers have discovered that several species of animals exist out there. Some are adorable, and some are terrifying. Some are fierce and considered dangerous.

> **Vampire bats:** There are more than a thousand species of bats in the world today. Yes, bat! Those flying birds that also looks like

rats have more than 1000 specie. There is a vampire bat specie. These bats have sharp, pointed teeth like the real vampire. Yet, when they bite, the pain isn't felt because they numb it with saliva. These shady creatures can keep sucking their victim's blood for over twenty minutes. You wouldn't feel a thing!

➤ **Leafy sea-dragon:** Leafy dragons exist on the southern and western Australian coast. They are ornately camouflaged. They create an illusion of their environment and blend in. They do this even when swimming, making them difficult to spot.

➤ **Glass Frogs:** glass frogs are found in tropical rainforests with treetops. About 50-60 species of glass frogs exist in America and Southern Mexico. Glass frogs are sometimes called see-through frogs because of their look.

➤ **Sea Pen:** Sea pens are found on the seafloor. They exist in pretty different shades of yellow, dark orange, and white. They are about 40cm in height and are similar to the quill pen. When touched, the sea pen glows a greenish shine.

➤ **Goblin Shark:** goblin sharks are rare, and they live 330 feet below the ground. They pose no threat to humans since they live so deep away.

➤ **Blue Parrotfish:** the blue parrotfish was found in the Atlantic Ocean. It spends most of its time searching for prey in the water. Looks like it is always hungry.

➤ **Red-lipped Batfish:** these fish are hardly seen as they are always on the bottom of the ocean. One weird fact about this fish is that it is a bad swimmer. Rather than swimming, the red-lipped Batfish walks in the ocean with pectoral fins.

➤ **Bush viper:** this specie of viper is found in tropical forests of Africa. They are spotted only at night when they go hunting.

Animal facts you should know

➤ **Chameleons have a very long tongue.** Their tongue is as long as their body. They use their tongue to capture their meals.

➤ **Earthworms have neither male nor female**. So how do they reproduce? Each earthworm is a male and a female altogether. However, they cannot reproduce by themselves. It takes two to tango. Two earthworms must come together to make the babies.

➤ **Giraffes are almost like humans, but only with their neck bones.** Giraffes have the same seven bones in the neck as humans. The only difference is there's are much larger than humans.

➤ **Eagles have sharp eyes.** Their eyes are four times sharper than humans. Another animal with close quality is the jaguar. A jaguar has eyes that can see six times better in the dark.

➤ **Polar bears have colorless hairs.** When you see a polar bear another time, look closely. It's easy to think the hairs are, but when in fact, they are not. What goes on there is a reflection of light by the hollow hairs.

➤ **Starfish have the highest survival rate.** You can split a starfish into quarters, and it still wouldn't die. As long as each piece has a part of the central disc, the fish continues to live. If you cut the fish without the central disc, it dies.

➢ **Hummingbirds hover at several flaps.** The hummingbird must flap its wings 180-200 times in a second to be able to over. How amazing and dangerous. It means if the hummingbird fails to make 180 flaps in just a second, it cannot hover. Yet, this bird hovers a lot. How many flaps do you think it takes to hover for a minute?

➢ **Owls hoot in pairs.** The next time you hear the hooting sound from owls, listen again. Better still, try to peek. You will see that there are two owls making the sound. The male owl does the actual hooting. The female owl twits.

➢ **Lions make the loudest roar in the cat family.** First, yes, lions belong to the cat specie. And unlike the common cat that meows in the home, lions roar. And their roars are the loudest. Their roars can be heard miles and miles away. About 3miles away.

➢ **Sloths are slow.** You won't blame them when you realize their food has been digest in two weeks. That would weaken anyone. Don't be slothful!

➢ **Cows make friends with themselves.** It's funny, but it's the truth. Cows befriend themselves. When they do, it's best not to separate them. The besties become stressed when separated.

➢ **Horses and cows are heavy sleepers** like these giant beings can sleep while standing. How relaxed! Much worse are the

Walruses. Those sleep for 19 hours a day. What time is left other than eating, and going back to bed?

- **Camels drink a lot!** Take a camel to a river or any water source, and it will drink about 50 liters of water. It doesn't even matter that the water is salty. The camel will continue to drink.

- **Dolphins conserve water.** Dolphins jump out of water in a bid to conserve water. They can move better in the air than in water.

- **Rats laugh.** You can make a rat laugh. All you need to do is pick one, tickle it, and have an ear out for its laughter.

- **Octopuses have nine brains and three hearts.** What they need nine brains remains a mystery, but they have all nine. And not just that, these species also have three hearts. Weird, really. Similar to this is the cows with four stomachs!

- **Sharks have the sixth sense**. Their sixth sense helps them to spot impulses with their muscle easily. The sixth sense is the electro-receptive.

- **Sea otters are romantic.** These sea animals sleep holding hands. But it's not for a romantic reason. It's a safety hack, so they don't drift apart.

- **Pigeons are important to chicks.** The male and female pigeons are food factories for babies (chicks). The pigeons produce crop milk which they use to feed their chicks.

- **Horseshoe crab has blue blood.** The blood of this particular specie of crab is unlike any blood. It is actually blue, not red.

- **Humans and chimpanzee have close DNA yet differ greatly.** Humans have been researched to have a close DNA with the chimpanzee. The percentage is almost a hundred (98%). One would think this makes humans and chimpanzees almost the same. Not true. Scientist believes there are at least a 34million differences between humans and chimpanzee.

How well do you know the Elephants?

An Elephant is easily one of the largest mammals on Earth. The tallest Elephant is 13 feet tall with body weight ranging from 4000-6000kg. Its trunk alone weighs 140kg. Its skin is 2.25cm thick. The Elephant uses its trunk to pick up items, comfort its calf and push things. It can also be used as a deadly weapon. The Elephant has two tusks which are elongated incisor teeth. The tusks start growing from the age of two. So, calves have tusks. The tusk isn't as heavy as the trunk, but they are close in range. An elephant's tusk weighs over 100kg. Thousands of elephants have been lost due to tusk extraction by man. Man continues to hunt them down. Their population, estimated at a little over 1.25 million, is now at 400,000.

One amazing fact about the Elephant is it never forgets. But there is much more to know about them. Below are more fun facts about an elephant:

❖ The largest mammal on Earth is the African Elephant. The Asian elephants are smaller than the African elephants.

❖ Out of the 24 hours that exist in a day, the Elephant spends more than half of it eating. An elephant eats for sixteen hours a day.

❖ Inside an elephant trunk is over 20,000 muscles.

❖ An elephant tusk, when cut off, doesn't grow back. That's just like losing a permanent tooth. It doesn't grow back.

❖ An elephant carries its pregnancy to term for twenty-two months. That means the Elephant has been pregnant for close to two years.

❖ Elephants are strong animals. The baby elephant can stand on its feet twenty minutes after its birth.

❖ Interestingly, these big babies are plant eaters. They do not eat flesh. They feed on bamboo, leaves, flowers, seeds, and fruits.

Amazing facts about Shark

Sharks have been in existence for millions of years. They live in water, and there are about 450-475 species of Shark. Sharks are fast swimmers. These boneless swimmers have no problem going into a trance. Just flip a shark upside down, and they go off on you, sleeping like they have been drugged. This effect is known as tonic immobility. Scientists use this method when working on species of fish. Once they are flipped and facing up, the fish goes into a trance. It's safer for everyone that way.

❖ Humans are not Shark's direct food. They don't go hunting for humans as meals. Seals, dolphins, and other big sea animals are their food. When a shark attacks a human, it is mostly an accident. It is more in defense than a hunting attack.

❖ Sharks have no bones. Their skeleton is a web of cartilage. Their skin also looks like sandpaper. However, the skin is full of tiny teeth structures called placoid scales. While swimming, the tail points in the tail's direction and help to reduce friction from the surrounding water.

❖ At night, sharks have improved vision. They can even see colors. Scientists were curious about this, and they studied the Shark. The discovery was found on the back of their eyes. The Shark's eyeball has a tapetum! The tapetum is a reflective layer that helps it see dimly lit areas.

❖ Sharks have a lifespan of twenty-five years, with some living up to a hundred years.

❖ The hammerhead shark has an odd head shape. The head shape, however, helps it see clearly. Nine species of hammerhead shark are known to exist all over the world. The hammerhead is heavy, weighing 1000lbs. It is also as long as 20 feet.

Dinosaurs

Dinosaurs are reptiles. They belong to the lizard family. These reptiles belong to one of the nearly extinct animals on the planet. There are more than 600 species of an extinct dinosaurs. A specie of dinosaurs has the longest name. The name is Micro pachycephalosaurus. The name means 'tiny thick-headed lizard.' And this animal is one to love. Here's why:

❖ Dinosaurs remain the biggest animal to have walked on Earth. A species of dinosaur named sauropod was discovered, and scientist confirmed that this animal remains the largest ever to walk on the Earth. Sauropod weighs between 69-72 tons and is 105-120 feet long.

- ❖ Some dinosaurs need to swallow big rocks so the rocks can grind their food.

- ❖ Based on the shape of their hip bone, there are two types of dinosaurs; Argentinosaurus, which are the heaviest. Quetzalcoatlus is the biggest.

- ❖ Dinosaurs have small brains. As they grew bigger and bigger, their brain chose to remain a cutie. A newborn human child has a bigger brain than an adult dinosaur.

The fascinating fly creatures

Birds are intriguing animals. Their best feature could be the ease with which they leave their current location for another. When their current location doesn't suit them, they hop and leave for another country. Quite an adventurous spirit they've got. It's easy to call them travelers. These creatures would drop everything for a better life out there. The better life could be the search for favorable weather, food, or even better accommodation. Birds travel in a large groups called flocks. The flocks are always the same species.

- **Numerous species:** more than ten thousand (10,000) species of birds exist. Each specie is unique in its color, features, and shape.

- **Birds make for good communicators:** birds' chip for several reasons. One of this is to pass along a message. Other times, the female bird chirps to attract her male counterpart. Some birds are great imitators. They can mimic humans to the teeth.

An example is the crows and ravens. And, of course, Parrot talks. It says what you say back to you. Birds also chip or sing to warn others of impending danger or to scare off a predator.

- **Every bird lays eggs:** birds lay eggs. Their young ones are hatched from the eggshells. They build a nest to lay their eggs safely and keep their eggs warm. This is important for the chicks to come to maturity.

- **Birds swallow their food:** they have no teeth, so every meal is swallowed. Their gizzard helps to grind their food into a smooth blend for easy digestion.

- **The bee hummingbird is the smallest:** bee hummingbirds are the smallest of birds. They are as small as 5cm in length. Their weight ranges between 1-2 grams.

The human body

The human body is another fascinating topic. Humans are equipped with the best of everything. This is what makes us a higher animals. The body is made in a way that is both interesting and hinges on perfection! Everything is thoroughly cut and shaped by an amazing sculptor. The human body is made up of billions of cells. The cells come together to form a mass of tissues. Tissues come together and form organs, and organs make up the body systems. Cells are the smallest living units in the body. We have cells all over the body responsible for performing varying functions.

The Human Cells

Life begins with every living being from a singular cell. The cell splits into half, each having what it takes to carry on with the reproduction. The division of a cell is growth. As the cell divides, growth begins. When it splits into half, each half has a nucleus. The nucleus is the core of a cell. When present, the cell is a complete unit. The half cells then split into different halves. That makes it two halves now, making a total of four cells. The four cells all can reproduce since they have nuclei in them. When these four cells divide, you have eight cells. And the division goes on and on.

A cell has three parts: the membrane, nucleus, and cytoplasm. The cell membrane is the outer covering of the cell. It controls what goes in and out of the cell. The nucleus is the life force of the cell. It dictates the genetic composition of the cell. It's where the body's DNA and RNA are. The cell performs numerous functions, ranging from carrying the heritable traits from parents to their offspring to protecting the body, and many more. To understand the impact of this micro unit of life, grouping the cells and learning what they do helps. The trillion cells in the body can be grouped into four (4). They are:

a) **Epithelial Cells** are tightly packed cells. They are the cells spread over the blood vessels, digestive organs, and surface body parts like the skin. Epithelial cells make it possible to have skin over our bodies. They ensure that we have protective skin, a protective layer on our blood, and a stomach to house our food.

b) **Nerve cells** are the cells involved in communication. They are sensitive cells that receive signal from the brain as information. The signal is passed to the muscles and glands to aid their ability to function. Most often, the signals that the nerve cells get from the brain tell these glands what to do. The nerve cells not only receive and send the brain's signal, but they also get signals from other body parts. For instance, the nerve cells get sensory information from the eyes, ears, and skin it to the brain. What nerve cells do is receive information from the brain to the body parts. Then they take back information from the body parts back to the brain. The nerve cells give us control over our bodies.

c) **Muscle cells** are the cells involved in the contraction and expansion of the muscle. Movement is possible because of nerve cells. The muscle cells pull and tug on the bones. They do the same pull and tug motion on the tendons. This is how they produce motion in the body. Muscle cells make up the thicker layer of blood vessels and digestive organs.

d) **Connective Tissue cells** are the cells concerned with the body structure. They give strength and rigidity. The tissue cells are also in charge of defending the body against invaders such as bacteria.

Cells make up the living tissue in man. Tissues make up the organs and then the system. The human body is a mass of organs formed from organs coming together. The human body is formed from trillions of cells rapidly. The body can be divided into three major parts:

1. **The head:** the part of the body that belongs to this part are: the forehead, eye, nose, mouth, tongue, teeth, jaw, ear, neck, chin, and cheek. The head serves as the protective bone for the skull. We see, talk, eat, listen, and smell because these body parts are on the head. The head also houses the brain, which is the powerhouse of the body, aside from the heart, of course. The bones of the head are twenty-two (22). The human head weighs between 2.0-5.0 kg, and sits proudly on the neck, supported by the vertebrae. Because the heart pumps blood and it is beneath, not above the head, one may ask how the head gets its blood supply. Well, there are arteries. They transport blood and other fluid to every body part, including the head.

2. **The trunk:** the trunk is the part of the body from the neck down. The backbone supports the human body. Without the backbone,

THE MOST AWESOME FACTS FOR CURIOUS KIDS

no vertebrate would be able to stand. The backbone, also known as the spine or spinal cord, is made from bones. These bones are called vertebrae. A spine has twenty-six (26) bones in them. These include the chest, stomach, back, shoulder, ribcage, bum, and private region. There is the chest cavity. The chest is part of the body between the neck and abdomen. The chest houses the breastplate. After the chest is the abdomen. Abs, or muscles cover the abdominal wall. The ribs surround the chest. The ribcage protects the heart, lungs, and other internal organs.

3. **The limbs:** these are the extremities in the body. The limbs can be divided into two: the lower and upper limbs. The upper region's limbs are located on the upper human body. They are; shoulder, arm, elbow, forearm, wrist, hands, and fingers. The upper limbs help to provide smooth movement of the upper body. They help maintain reflexes and tone. The lower limbs are the extremities on the lower body parts. They include: the hip, buttocks, leg, thigh, knee, calf, ankle, foot, heel, and toes. Without the lower limb, there would be no movement from one place to another. The lower limbs also provide support for the body weight.

Aside from the common features of the body, awesome facts about these body parts exist. For instance, the food we eat takes close to twelve hours to digest in the body. When you eat, the food doesn't immediately digest. It sits in the body for twelve hours with enzymes and the digestive system working on it. The unneeded food is passed out as feces.

The heart is another interesting organ, which pumps blood to every body part and beats about a hundred thousand (100,000) times daily. In a year, the heart would have beat three million, six hundred and fifty thousand (3,650,000) times. An adult male's heart weighs 300g, and female's weighs 250g. A baby's heart weighs 100g.

The Human System

The human body is a mass of systems. A system is an assembly of varying organs that performs specific functions. There are ten major body systems.

1. The Skeletal System

The human body has shape and structure because of the bones supporting it. You can feel the bones in your body. They are everywhere, in the head, the hands, the leg, the back, everywhere. What do you think the body would look like without these bones? The human body without bones would look like a heap of sand. There would be no bone backbone supporting movement. The head wouldn't be able to stand or sit right. The head wouldn't be sitting right on the neck because there would be no bone to hold it. We would all be bags of sand. So, bones play important roles in human life. They give structure and support to the human body. The bones of the body are referred to as the skeleton. An adult has 200 bones in its skeletal system.

2. Muscular System

Every human has not less than six hundred and fifty (650) muscles. These muscles attach tendons to the skeleton. Muscles make movement smooth and without restriction. Even the skeleton needs muscles to work right and provide movement. Muscles work in two ways. They work voluntarily when it is the human controlling their movement. The involuntary muscles work without any conscious effort from humans. These include the cardiac muscle involved in pumping blood and the smooth muscles that maintain blood flow and pressure. The muscular system is majorly in three groups, each serving its purpose where it is located. The first is the skeletal muscles. These muscles make up about 40% of human weight. Aside from giving us structure and shape, bones also constitute our body weight.

The second muscular system is the cardiac muscle. These muscles are found within the heart. They are involuntary muscles involved in the pumping and circulation of blood. The pumping occurs in the heart, and the muscles circulate that blood to other body parts.

The third group of the muscular system is the smooth muscle. Smooth muscles are found in the urinary bladder, digestive tract, gallbladder, veins, and arteries. These muscles are another example of involuntary muscles. Their movement cannot be controlled.

Generally, muscles work in pairs. They are well coordinated to produce movement and other reflex actions in a process called Antagonism. This means they work in opposites. When one muscle contrast, the other expands like an antagonist. The movement is entirely friendly, not a battle. The pairing is needed.

3. Nervous System

The nervous system plays a vital role in the human body. This system is the body's smart chip. It coordinates our actions. It is involved in how we respond to touches, shock, and signals. The nervous system does this by transmitting the signals to different parts of the body and from them. This system is sensitive enough to pick even the slightest change in the environment. It then helps the response to such changes with the help of the endocrine system.

The feeling is possible because of the nervous system. We can feel when we are pricked. We can explain a burning sensation because the nervous plays its role right. It is involved in processing and thinking patterns. It plays a crucial role in our ability to retain memory.

The nervous system consists of the central and peripheral nervous systems. The central nervous system consists of the brain and spinal cord. This system is in charge of sending information from one part of the body to the other. While it sends the information, this organ sends back the information it receives from the recipient part. The peripheral nervous system consists of the spinal and cranial nerves. The role of the peripheral is majorly taking care of signals related to movement. It controls processes like breathing and heartbeat. Like the central nervous system, the peripheral system also sends and receives the signal.

4. Cardiovascular System

The cardiovascular system is the circulatory system. The heart and vessels make up the heart. The heart is the pumping machine, and the vessels, which include veins, arteries, and capillaries, transport this blood to every body part. Without the circulatory system, blood cannot reach vital body parts. This will eventually result in death as blood is the fuel that keeps the body functioning. As the blood flows through vital organs, it also carries nutrients. These are nutrients gotten from food and fruits. The cardiovascular system also helps the body maintain a stable temperature. This happens with the continuous blood flow alongside nutrients to every cell in the body.

5. Lymphatic System

The lymphatic system is involved in the regulation of blood flow. When excess blood is in the body, the lymphatic system steps in. It returns the excess blood. About 80-90% of the blood is returned, and the remaining percentage becomes part of the interstitial fluid. This fluid is found surrounding tissue cells. Sometimes, the excess blood is unable to be returned safely. It happens when protein molecules leak into the bloodstream, causing osmotic pressure in the interstitial fluid. If the fluid continues to grow without an outlet, it results in swelling. The swelling is known as edema.

Aside from this, the lymphatic system absorbs fat and fat-soluble vitamins from the body. They then transport these nutrients to the vein.

The lymphatic system is also known for its defense against microorganisms and diseases. This is perhaps its best function yet. The lymphatic system contains lymphocytes that fight microorganisms and foreign bodies.

6. Respiratory System

It is commonly believed that the respiratory system is concerned with breathing. But there is more to the respiratory system than taking in oxygen and breathing it out. Breathing plays a major role in providing oxygen to the body. This gas is needed for metabolism. The cells need oxygen to keep functioning right. The respiratory system and circulatory system ensure the blood pH is well regulated.

7. Digestive System

The digestive system processes the food into smaller bits that the body can utilize. Food taken into the body is acted on by enzymes to stimulate digestion. Digestion begins from the mouth when the food is chewed. Saliva mingles with the food to bring about the quick breakdown. The food is then passed down to the digestive canal, consisting of a long pipe that extends to the anus from the mouth. The digestive system consists of the mouth, pharynx, esophagus, stomach, small intestine, and large intestine. The tongue, teeth, and saliva also play a role in food digestion. The teeth grind the food to a smooth texture. The saliva softens the food, and meat. And the whole movement happens on the tongue.

Food undergoes three major procedures in the body: digestion, absorption, and elimination. After the food is consumed through the mouth, it is passed down to the digestive tract for digestion. Afterward, digestion begins. Digestion can be mechanical or chemical. Mechanical digestion involves chewing the food until it has been grounded to finer particles. Enzymes in the saliva (lysozymes, amylases, lipases) act on it. This aids its quick absorption by the body. Chemical digestion involves the digestion of food through the use of water and digestive enzyme in a process called hydrolysis. This is a faster means of digestion as the digestive enzymes speed up the process. Chemical digestion works for carbohydrates, proteins and fats with complex molecules.

After digestion, the body absorbs the needed part of the food. The cell membranes allow the passage of the digested food into the blood or lymph. The excess food, that cannot be digested, is then passed out as waste. The waste can be urine or feces and passed out of the body through the anus.

8. Endocrine System

The endocrine system is a network of organs and glands responsible for releasing hormones into the bloodstream. Endocrine uses these hormones to control your moods, body mechanism, reproduction, development, and growth. How you respond to stress, injury, and your mood depends on the Endocrine system.

The hormones released are chemical messengers. They affect and help control the body's processes. Most times, the processes in the body require more than one hormone acting. The body uses hormones to communicate its need to the appropriate channel. If the body needs water, for example, the body secretes the vasopressin hormone. This hormone alerts the kidney of water shortage in the body. The kidneys take the signal and start to conserve water. The result is that less urine is passed out.

The body communicates using hormones in two ways. The first is to let state its need for two glands of the same organ simultaneously. What happens here is when the hormone is activated, one increases its production rate, and the other slows down. This process is noticed in the pituitary and thyroid gland. The thyroid-stimulating hormone released by the pituitary gland triggers the thyroid gland to release its hormone. The secretion of TSH pushes the thyroid gland to release the hormone that affects the body.

Another way the body communicates using hormones is to use the endocrine and another gland. For instance, the pancreas releases insulin. The insulin acts on muscles and the liver to process glucose.

The organs of the Endocrine system include the male testes, the female ovaries, the pituitary gland, and the adrenal glands. Each of these glands secretes hormone, which the Endocrine system releases into the body. The hormones released by the Endocrine system include:

a. **Pituitary Gland:** Prolactin, Growth hormone, Adrenocorticotropic hormone, Prolactin, Luteinizing hormone, Follicle-stimulating hormone, Antidiuretic hormone, oxytocin.

b. **Adrenal Glands:** Cortisol, Aldosterone, Adrenaline, Noradrenaline.

c. **Ovaries:** Estrogen, Progesterone, Testosterone.

d. **Testes:** testosterone.

Hormones control lots of bodily processes. They control the body's metabolism, mood, homeostasis, temperature, sexual function, reproduction, growth, and development. And as little as a slight change in the level of any of the hormones in the body can cause significant changes. Sometimes, this results in health complications, diseases, or ailments. Thus, hormonal levels must be kept in balance.

9. Urinary System

The urinary system is in charge of riding the body of wastes, basically urine. This system helps keep body liquid's level and composition in check. The urinary system controls the production of red blood cells. It does this by secreting erythropoietin. The urinary system is not the only organ involved in the excretion of waste products. Others, such as the respiratory system, take out carbon dioxide as waste gas. The skin secretes sweat as a waste products. However, as these organs have their role, so does the urinary tract. It keeps the fluid volume in check by excreting the excess as urine.

10.   Reproductive System

The reproductive system is concerned with reproduction. This is the process involved in the birthing of human babies. Before birth, reproductive organs start to develop to maturity. Women have different reproductive organs separate from men, just like the body differs. The reproductive organ in a woman are ovaries, fallopian tubes, uterus, cervix, and vagina. In a man, the prostate, testes, and penis are the reproductive organs.

For reproduction to happen, the male must produce sperm which will fertilize the eggs from the female. Reproduction is an internal process. The sperm cells travel along the female's vagina, through the cervix, and into the uterus. The sperm continues its journey into the fallopian tube to fertilize the egg, also known as the ovum. A successful fertilization results in a fertilized egg, now a zygote traveling to implant itself properly in the uterine wall. Thus begins the gestation period known as the pregnancy stage.

The female carries her child(ren) to the term for nine months. Nine months, the baby grows from a small egg fertilized to an embryo.

Below are more cool facts about the human body:

∞ The human body grows rapidly within the first two years of birth. This explains why babies grow so fast.

∞ Man needs three basic things for survival: air, water, and food in that order. Without oxygen, there is no life. Humans can still survive on water for days without food. An average human can live for only three minutes without air. We can survive 3-5 days without water. And we can go hungry for 40 days without dying. These are in the extreme cases. Please, do not attempt to do it.

∞ 20% of the oxygen we breathe in is used up by the brain. The brain needs oxygen to function properly. During oxygen deprivation, the brain suffers it most. The condition where the brain is starved of oxygen is called cerebral hypoxia. This results in an emergency that must be tended to immediately. If not treated, oxygen deprivation of the brain can cause brain damage or death. Cerebral hypoxia doesn't just happen. It is caused by choking, drowning, accident, head injury, or suffocation. The brain cannot go more than five minutes without oxygen.

∞ The human ear and nose grow all through life. They do not stop growing. As we age, the other body parts shrink but not those two. The answer to this awesome fact is that the nose and ear are made of cartilage cells. These cells divide more as they age. And do the ear and nose grow bigger than the body? No, they don't. The growth is in a bit.

∞ Aside from humans' unique fingerprints, we also have distinct tongue prints. The DNA makes up for that. That is what sci-fi and regular movies do when they take a suspect's cup for forensic investigation. Even the tongue has something to say about you.

∞ The human brain is three times bigger than other animals. This could be why we have more developed brains and the ability to think. Animals do not!

∞ The largest muscle is located in the bum. It is called *'gluteus maximus,',* and it helps when we lift our legs. The smallest muscle is the *'stapedius.'* It is found in the mid-ear. It helps to keep the smallest bone in the body stable.

∞ An adult has 206 bones. A baby has over 300 bones. The bones fuse as the baby grows until the child become an adult. And the number of bones is 206.

Weird places in the world

The world is beautiful, so many things about it aren't yet known. There are beautiful places to want to see definitely. There are also certain places you will not believe exist. Places you would rather not want to check out. Adventurers stumble on some of these places by chance. After their discovery, though, it was seen that some sites make for a good tourist centers.

Giant Causeway in Northern Ireland.

If you love a volcanoes tour, then the Giant Causeway will interest you. Volcanic eruptions are upward plumes of sparks. They happen when the Earth becomes too hot for comfort. It can be extremely hot within the Earth and some rocks start to melt. As they melt, they become a thick flowing substance called magma or lava. The magma is very light and eventually erupts from the Earth's surface. There's been no less than 1500 volcanoes in the world, each differing. In Northern Ireland, a volcanic eruption happened sixty million years ago. A huge chunk of molten basalt erupted out of the Earth with a huge volcano. The basalt solidified and started to contract while cooling off. The effect of this was cracks that are visible to date. Over 35,000 polygon columns exist at the Giant Causeway, believed to have been created by giants. This is one of the weirdest places on Earth.

Pamukkale in Turkey

In Southwest Turkey, is a mineral-rich hot fluid flowing down the valley side in ridges. Pamukkale is a geological delight. Travelers who love a touch of geographical history in places they visit would love this place. The beauty is surrounded by Hierapolis, which is like an ancient spa city in Rome. Hierapolis was discovered in the 1900s but is now in ruins. You will find a pristine theatre and tombs in this Hierapolis. The combination of Pamukkale and Hierapolis makes a great tourist site.

An interesting thing to know about Pamukkale is that it is more than 100m high. It is so high that residents of Denzili, who are about 20km away, can see it. Also, the water flowing in this spring is hot, and the temperature ranges from 36-100degree centigrade. It is worth noting also that Pamukkale got its name from the Turkish translation of cotton castle. This is a reflection of its appearance. It is called a cotton castle because it looks like a cotton plantation.

The pool in Pamukkale is believed to be Cleopatra's pool. The Turkish believed that the Egyptian Queen swam there. Pamukkale hosts over two million visitors annually.

Lake British Columbia in Canada

The spotted lake in Canada to date is considered a sacred lake. The lake is said to be sacred due to the therapeutic waters that come out of it. In summer, the water from the lake evaporates, leaving small mineral pools behind. Each mineral deposit is different from the next. During the first world war, the spotted lake was used in making ammunition.

THE MOST AWESOME FACTS FOR CURIOUS KIDS

Visitors are hardly allowed near the sacred lake. The lake can, however, be seen from Highway 3 Northwest of Osoyoos. And it remains a breathtaking site.

Thor's Well in the USA

In Oregon, USA is a natural hole that looks like it's draining the sea. This well is a natural wonder because its ground can't be seen. It is thus called bottomless and dangerous. Researchers claim that the well started as a sea cave that was a result of a wave. The cave roof especially fell to create an opening at the bottom of the ocean. Thor's well is not a site to be during sudden torrents. The torrents can sweep off unsuspecting visitors into the well. However, the best time to visit the well is an hour preceding the high tide. It's the best time to see it without water and witness its formation as it fills up.

Pico de Fogo in Cape Verde

This is the highest point in Cape Verde. It is also the highest peak in Africa. Pico rises over 9,000 feet above sea level. It is believed to be an active stratovolcano within the Island of Fogo. Fogo in Portuguese means *"fire,"* a perfect description of the hotspot volcanic island. The main cone of Pico last erupted in 2014 after the last eruption in 1995. The eruption in 1995 happened on April 3. It covered the Island with an ash cloud. The eruption was similar to small earthquakes, as reported by the residents. The earthquakes began six days earlier. The homes of the residents were destroyed. They had to evacuate from their home.

Mount Vesuvius in Italy

Italy houses one of the most famous volcanoes in the world. Mount Vesuvius is the most dangerous volcano with its past eruptions. In 79 AD, the volcanic eruption from this mount destroyed Pompeii and Herculaneum completely. Again, in 1906, new lava from the mount resulted in the deaths of over 200 people. Visitors of Mount Vesuvius can hike and peer around it, but extreme caution must be taken. Among other things, the mount has a deceiving appearance.

The Red Beach in Greece

Yes, a red beach in Santorini makes it one of the weirdest places in the world. Santorini beach used to be an active volcano. Its past eruptions gave the Island its famous reddish beach and shape. It also has red and black rocks that give it an eccentric look. The huge red cliff that hangs over the clear blue water gives Santorini beach its famous

The Stone Forest in China

The Shilin, also called the stone forest, is located in the Yunnan province in China. This forest has no trees. Not a single one. All there is in the forest are stones. The stone forest used to be a shallow sea millions of years ago. The Shilin forest is 150 square meters with great and small stones. It also has a cave called Zhiyun. There are two lakes, too: Lake Change and lake Yue.

World Mysteries

Some events are flagged as mysterious when researchers have no proof or logical explanation. Some of these mysteries range from historical places, sites, monuments, or even tombs of famous people. And some are fables invented that scientists have no proof if are true or not. Below are world mysteries that remain unsolved to date.

- King Arthur

If you watched the movie; Merlin, you'd want to meet or know more about King Arthur. The story of King Arthur and his great accomplishment in Camelot is intriguing. The stories further state his knights, and the round table talks. There is also his wizard, Merlin, and the numerous battles they conquered. King Arthur's stories talk about his people loving him so much. Yet, if this King exists, there's no proof of it. Researchers found evidence insisting that King Arthur was from Tintagel in Britain. Yet, when excavators arrived, none of the exhumes proved that this King lived and died there. Apparently, this King may be more of an invention than a reality. However, so much has been heard about this infamous King to discard that he doesn't exist. Scholars are keeping their fingers crossed until the next piece of evidence turns up to prove his existence.

- **The money pit on Oak Island**

Another widely circulated story is the money pit in Oak Island Nova Scotia, in Canada. It is believed that the pirate Captain William Kidd buried a large amounts of money worth millions of dollars on Oak Island.

Movies sometimes throw too much limelight on these stories that they appear almost true. The series on "*The curse of Oak Island*" has left people wondering if there isn't some money pit buried in Oak Island. Even President Roosevelt wanted to know if this was true. The search for this supposed money pit has been on for centuries now. Yet, no money pit has been discovered on the Island. But the Island in itself exists. Also, there is a dented look on it.

Some group of friends discovered this dent, about 100ft deep. What these men went to do on the Island remains unclear. It is safe to say that they had gone to check for themselves the missing money. Perhaps, mother luck would shine on them, and they would find what others have failed to see. The men started digging, and they dug until they were exhausted. They found nothing!

- **The Ark of Covenant**

In the years before Christ, king Nebuchadnezzar and his Babylonian army conquered Jerusalem. After the conquest, the army took their spoils home. One of their spoils was the Ark of Covenant from the Temple. In this Ark was the ten-commandment written on two tablets. No one knows where the Ark is. Some stories claimed the Ark never made it to Babylon and was hidden before the city was captured. Another source claimed the Ark did get to Babylon, but that Jerusalem reclaimed it. Researchers and Scholars have a hard time locating the Ark, which is neither in Jerusalem nor Babylon. Some schools believe the Ark will never be found as it was never meant to be. And that until the Messiah arrives, there would be no Ark.

- ## City of Atlantis

A popular story in the fourth century in Greece was the story of the city of Atlantis. The city was believed to exist in the Atlantic Ocean, and it conquered Europe and Africa. According to the story, the Athenians fought back when the city of Atlantis waged war against it. The result was Atlantis being engulfed by the waves. Scholars do not believe the story. However, they believe the story could be linked to Greek real-life incidence at the time. A similar event is a Minoan civilization located on the Island of Crete. The story of the Minoans is that the Mycenaeans conquered them.

- ## The Holy Grail

The Holy Grail is another mystery. The grail is the cup Jesus Christ used at the last supper while dining with his disciples. No one paid attention to this cup until the mid-ages. The king Arthur story may have also disregarded the interest in this cup. The Holy grail was one of the quests for the knights of Camelot in one of the episodes of Merlin. Other stories of the King Arthur also referenced the Holy Grail. Scholars have not attempted to search for this cup. Perhaps if they do, they might find the Holy Grail.

Cool kids who are inventors

Children can be anything they want to be. Children have the power to be who they want to be. And they have adults to help with their bidding. Children can do a whole lot more, and nothing's stopping them. Not even age. The following are kids who invented some cool things at a young age too. Today, they are credited with young innovators.

We love Popsicles, and Frank Epperson invented them

In 1905, eleven-year-old Frank Epperson accidentally made the world's first Popsicle. What happened? It was winter, and he wanted to make frozen fruit juice. He took out soda water powder and added water to make a concoction. After the mix, he took the bowl and went outside to enjoy the evening breeze with his family. And so, he forgot his drink overnight outside.

Frank saw that his concoction had become a frozen mixture the next morning. He tried it and loved the taste. And there goes the first Popsicle in the world. Loving the frozen mix, Frank went on making his Popsicle at home. No one noticed this, though, until 1922 when he gave it out as a gift at a Fireman's ball. That was seventeen years later. Everyone who had a taste loved it. People started to ask for more. And the mass production of Popsicle began. The name he called his frozen mix was *Eppsicle*. But his children started calling it Popsicle. So, Frank Epperson chose the name Popsicle. Funny how he invented his Popsicle as a child and only got to make them as an adult. However, his children naming his Eppsicle as popsicles was a cliché.

Swim Flippers make us swim better, thanks to Ben Franklin

Also, at eleven, Ben Franklin made an amazing invention. Ben Franklin has gained recognition mostly for what he accomplished as an adult. Yet, this man was an inventor at eleven. He started his mission early, it would seem. In the 1700s, Ben, while swimming, discovered something huge. He realized you could swim better if the water's surface area is wide enough to push through. He invented handheld fins that he made out of planks. He put holes in the middle of the design of the hand and feet. The modern-day flippers for swimmers are a chip of the young chap's novel invention. Ben Franklin's other inventions include a Lightning rod, Flexible catheter, 24-hour wheel-clock, Glass armonica, Bifocals, and long arm extension, but not as a child. His second invention came 24 years later.

Who loves to jump on the Trampoline? George Nissen thought it was cool!

The Trampoline was invented by sixteen-year-old George Nissen. In 1930, while watching a performance by the Trapeze artists, George watched as the artist dropped on a net. As he walked home that night, he thought the performance would have been better if the drop act was on a bouncing something rather than net. He got home and started his theory in his parents' garage. His first product was made with metal, and a canvas spread over it. He continued to improve his design and replaced the canvas with a nylon canvas. The effect is more bounce.

Louise Braille makes us see with his Braille invention

Louise Braille wasn't born blind. But at the young age of three, he lost sight to an eye infection. Reading was difficult for him. Unlike other children, he struggled to trace his letter with his fingers. He could never read properly using that method. The frustration on the little child was more than he could bear. When he turned twelve, Louise learned the silent communication method used by the French military. Viola! It worked for him. With that, Braille could read easily. He decided to improve on this approach for blind people who, like him, could not read with the finger tracing method. Today, Braille is widely used in blind schools. And he is known as the blind boy who invented his reading and writing format. Yet, he was a blind boy. There's so much you can do!

Sweeping is more fun with Sam Houghton's invention

In 2008, Mark Houghton submitted a patent application for his child. As he was sweeping the yard two years back, his son had watched him sweeping with two brooms. The three-year-old then thought there should be a better way to do it. What Sam did next impress his father. The child picked the two brooms and joined them with a rubber band. It was a seemingly simple attempt. But coming from a three-year-old, it was a thoughtful insight. Mark, a patent advisor, saw this as something worthy of note. He got the patent form for his son naming him as the singular inventor of the idea. The application was granted in

2008, and Sam was five by then. The patent was awarded to Sam Houghton for his two-headed sweeper device. And though the association doesn't record age, they were impressed that a five-year-old became an inventor.

Philo Farnsworth and his cool television precursor

Philo Farnsworth was a farm boy who lived on a Utah farm. Whenever he had the chance, he would sit and watch the plows go back and forth. While watching, he made sketches borne out of the plow's movement that fascinated him so much. In 1921 shortly before Philo Farnsworth turned fifteen, he sketched a diagram for an electronic television system. Nothing was heard until his electronic sketch became a reality after six years. The image dissector was able to send out its first transmission. Today, that invention started off a series of other electronic inventions. Farnsworth himself went on to invent several other electronic devices, such as Fusor. Fusor is an apparatus that makes nuclear fusion. He was involved in developing an electron microscopes, infrared night vision, gastroscopes, radar, and baby incubators. In 1984, he was inducted into the National Inventors Hall of Fame.

Nothing makes us worried about a self-disinfecting hazmat suit

In 2014, when the Ebola scare was all everyone could think of, Nine-year-old Mark was Leschinsky seeing something else. The hazmat suit that the health workers wore had an issue. Something about the design didn't look right, considering 900 health workers got infected despite wearing it. Mark started to look for a way to help the health workers be protected. He figured if he could protect them, there would be more trained hands to help the sick people. So, the 9-year-old thought of making a self-disinfecting hazmat suit. And he did! Mark made a suit that had three layers. It also has an inner layer that is not penetrable. He then put a disinfecting solution at the center of the suit. It was a masterpiece. He went ahead to add external protection by adding a perforated layer. The layer allows the viruses on the suit to be killed. It's not surprising that a year later, Mark Leschinsky was welcomed into the National Gallery of Young Inventors.

Conclusion

There are awesome things to learn about the world, animals, space, and places. You have to know where to look and what you aim to achieve. Nurture your curiosity. Your curiosity is a gift that should be fanned, not locked up. The amazing things you see today exist in this book because someone was curious enough to want to know them. By exploring these options, we have answers to questions that plague our minds. By exploring, we discover hidden truths. By fanning our curiosity, we have amazing inventions and innovations. So, are you curious? Dig in! who knows, just what you might uncover? The future is yours for the taking! Seize it.

Hidden in the world, space, technology, science, and nature are treasure waiting to be discovered. There is no limit to how far you can go. The space provides us with such as the stars, moon, sun, and planetary bodies. Technology has shown us the highest levels of possibilities with their inventions. The world is filled with amazing creatures, waiting to be known and understood. Science gives opens up the doors of truth that we do not know exists. And nature has everything wrapped up in beautiful wraps. Are you curious about what all these holds for you? keep exploring, for in that lies the answer to your insatiable quench to know more.

Source Reference

1. Weird places in the world

   https://traveltriangle.com/blog/59-weirdest-places-across-the-world/

2. Amazing things you didn't know were invented by kids.

   https://www.mentalfloss.com/article/93162/11-inventions-made-kids

3. Interesting human body facts for kids

   https://www.google.com/amp/s/parenting.firstcry.com/articles/20-interesting-human-body-facts-for-kids/%3famp

4. Buffetaut E, Sueethorn V, Cuny G, Tong H, Le Loeuff J, Khansubha S, Jonngautchariyakul S. The earliest known sauropod Dinosaur. Nature. 20000 Sep 7;407(6800):72-74. [PubMed] [Google Scholar]

5. The Earth www.space.com

6. The space www.nasa.gov

7. Fact sheet: Benjamin Franklin's inventions.

   https://www.visitphilly.com/media-center/press-releases/fact-sheet-benjamin-franklin-inventions/

8. The human body www.healthline.com

9. Anatomy of the Endocrine System www.hopkinsmedicine.org

10.   Animal facts for kids. National Geographic kids

   www.natgeokids.com

THANK YOU

Hello there!

I wanted to take a moment to sincerely thank you for reading my book all the way through. I am so appreciative that you took the time to read my first book, which I poured my heart and soul into writing.

Please don't hesitate to email the following address if you have any comments or adjustments I can make to this publication or even to my future works:

publishing.improvement@gmail.com

Your suggestions would be really helpful to me.

I want to thank you once more for your support and wish you the same pleasure reading my book as I had writing it.

Best wishes.

Clifford McDaniel

Printed in Great Britain
by Amazon

23335009R00046